CARTOONS FROM PLAYBOY

SO THIS IS LOVE

by

Brian Savage

PAN BOOKS LTD : LONDON

First published 1971 simultaneously in the
United States of America and Canada by
Playboy Press, Chicago, Illinois.

This edition published 1972 by Pan Books Ltd,
33 Tothill Street. London, SW1.

ISBN 0 330 23183 9

2nd Printing 1972

*Printed in Great Britain
by Fletcher & Son Ltd, Norwich*

PREFACE

Brian Savage is an eligible bachelor-about-Manhattan whose first PLAYBOY cartoon appeared in the July 1961 issue. Since that time, his antic mind and breezy drawing style have given birth to some of the magazine's wittiest visual humour. He was born in Cambridge, Massachusetts, but prefers to live in New York, 'where I can whip around to the Metropolitan Museum once or twice a week'. His favourite cartoonist is George Price. The advantage of the cartoonist's life, he feels, is 'the sense of independence,' which he admits may be just another way of saying 'insecurity'. Another big advantage is therapy: 'I get a lot off my chest by doing cartoons'.

His name to the contrary, Mr Savage's art is not really savage. Pointed, perceptive, piquant, yes; uniquely critical of the attitudes and platitudes of contemporary life, definitely. But *savage* implies something violent and primitive, whereas the work of this talented man is civilized and urbane. There is something rather disarming about the judge who leans down from his lofty bench to lecherously suggest to the buxom chippie who has been brought before him, 'Let's talk about your getting time off for good behaviour'. And there is a touching expression on the face of the old gentleman who, while having his needs filled by a fetishistically attired lady, contentedly sighs the phrase which is the title of this present book: 'So this is love.' This kind of amused respect for the foibles of humanity is typical of his work and is not to be found in humourists who wield more vicious, less tolerant pens.

Linger no longer here, then, but turn the page and enter the wacky, wistful world of Brian Savage.

The editors of PLAYBOY

"My God, Ned, couldn't you wait until the Friday-night party?"

*"It's just as we suspected, gentlemen—
C ration is an aphrodisiac."*

"Of course I'm very flattered and pleased, but believe me, Kenneth, mother knows best."

"My God! Can't I take you anyplace without your embarrassing me?!"

*"Our talks were exceedingly cordial and fruitful.
In other words, we are at war."*

"You've built a better mousetrap, all right, but I can't help wondering at the practicality of the nuclear warhead."

"*What's the big problem? If you can't get along, get a divorce.*"

"Oh, the usual. What kind of day did <u>you</u> have?"

"*I've given you four years at Choate, four years at Princeton and three years at the Harvard Business School. Now I'm turning over the business to you. Of course it's bankrupt.*"

"*In the talent category, Miss Foster will recite a list of books she has read.*"

"*The court sentences you to, oh, four and a half years.*"

"The next time someone makes a heavy
pass, Miss Wickerly, you've simply got to
do more than go limp in protest."

"*For a brief moment, I thought we were witnessing the bright new dawn of a literary renaissance.*"

"*There should be no difficulty about the divorce, Mr. Briggs, but it never hurts to have the court on our side.*"

"Oddly enough, that's one of the few jokes he considers decent enough to tell in mixed company."

"*The most dedicated men in medicine are gynecologists. All they talk about is their work.*"

"Today you're going to march in there and ask for an increase in knowledge."

*"Give her the full starlet treatment—clipped,
capped, cupped, couched and cast . . . !"*

"*I can't help thinking, Ellen, suppose there isn't a life after death?*"

"*The meeting was called to order by the chairman. For two hours everyone compromised his personal integrity. A motion was made and seconded to adjourn the meeting. The meeting was adjourned.*"

"*It gets more commercial every year, doesn't it?*"

"I love the atmosphere in here."

"*Oh, Lord, I can act!*"

"*Here's our written consent. Are you joining the army? Getting married? Leaving the country? Or what?*"

"*There's a doctor's real reward, Wilcox. The sight of a patient on the mend.*"

"*For heaven's sake! Don't just stand there and
tell me about the law of the jungle!*"

"Whether you know it or not, buddy,
you've got a star on your hands!"

"I said, 'I, too, am a nonconformist.'"

"*That's the sort of thing that gives boxing a bad name.*"

"*That's the very same swashbuckling charm that won my heart over thirty years ago.*"

*"Are you crazy? Move out of the neighborhood
just when it's starting to deteriorate?"*

"*Inability to start on these dangerous wintry days is one of our safety features.*"

"*Now, today's graduate simply wouldn't understand that kind of school spirit.*"

"*Come in, sir, come in!*"

*"It's not as if I were looking for sex or drugs.
All I want is a lousy glass of beer."*

"*I love a parade . . . . !*"

"*It's my table, all right, but you're
just not my kind of people.*"

"*They're not exactly consulting physicians,
Miss Walters. As a matter of fact,
they're just some fellows I play golf with.*"

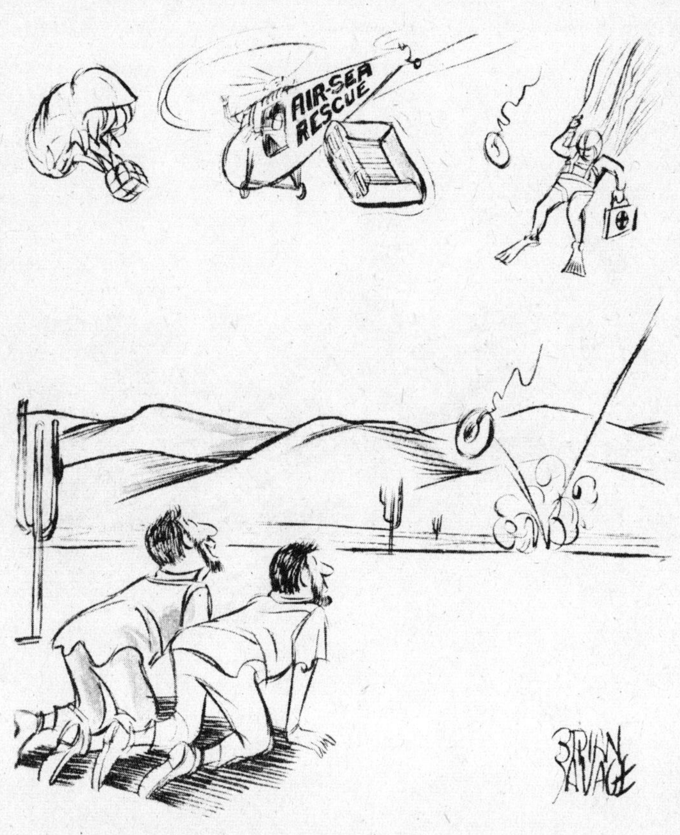

"*We're saved! We're saved! I think.*"

"*You'll never catch any waves with <u>that</u> rig, buddy.*"

"*It started years ago when Ogden sat down
next to this girl one morning and
realized he'd forgotten his newspaper.*"

"My lawyers will handle the fine print."

TELEVISION PRODUCTION
THE WONDERFUL WORLD OF

"*The passengers are all below, I trust.*"

"*That does it. No more Christmas parties until this place is fully automated.*"

"We're going into our landing pattern now. Would you like something to read?"

"A real gentleman. I've yet to hear him raise his voice in anger."

"*At least he was gentleman enough
to give me his seat!*"

"Now, your daddy won't have time to listen to what happens to you every day at school, but he definitely wants a report, a summation, if you will, when you get your college degree."

"*Let's show the pope where we stand!*
Let's get out there and get pregnant!"

"*Mini, midi, maxi, moe....*"

"*What do you suppose Alice used to get to Wonderland?*"

"Well, Betsy, I think it's about time
to move on to skydiving."

"Come now, Dr. Hubbell. All teachers, whether they want to admit it or not, have their favorites."

"*I can't shake the nagging feeling that this is part of a governmental plan to curb overseas spending.*"

*"How else is a girl going to meet a fellow
in New York?"*

OLYMPICS 68
GRINGOS
GRINGOS
GOS
BIPIN
SAVAGE

"*Well, we gambled and lost.*"

"I am the ghost of Christmas past."

"Harry's not having much luck with his
'Step outside for a cigarette and a breath
of fresh air' routine tonight."

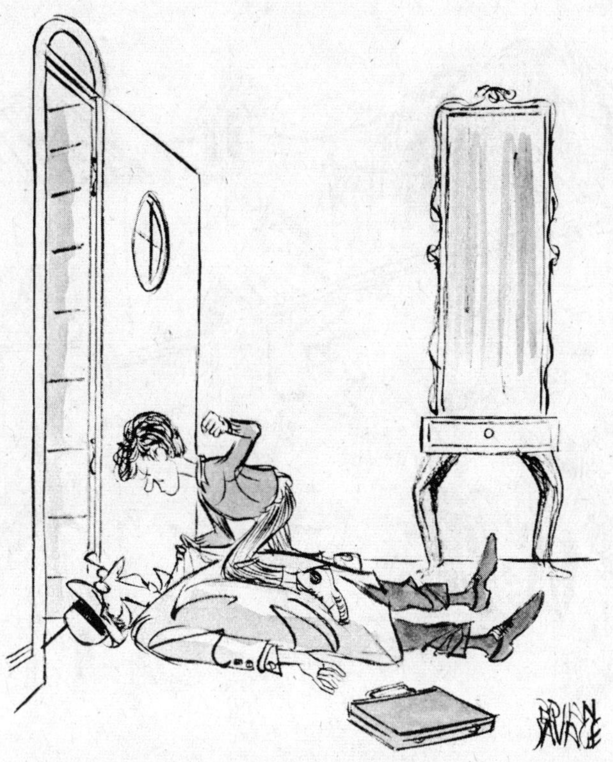

"You gladden my heart, Tom. Too many sons behave indifferently toward their dads."

"I don't suppose you'd care to hear
the rest of my inaugural address?"

"Just one question, Natalie. Do you love the guy?"

"*Actually, we're quite content. He's got his dirty books and I've got my gin.*"

*"I've never heard the senator make a
more emotional speech. Especially the part
about the cost of the time slot."*

"He's probably the finest grass-roots
campaigner in the country today."

"It's not so surprising when you consider that most accidents occur in the home."

"*You're fortunate to grow up in these exciting times—the breakup of the atom, the breakthrough of space exploration, the breakdown of morals. . . .*"

"*We make it a point not to stand on ceremony around here.*"

"The Board of Education requires me to give you
some basic information on sex, reproduction and
other disgusting filth."

"*This looks like an interesting case.*"

"Always remember, son, juvenile delinquency
don't start on any street corner.
It starts right here in the home!"

"*I move to admit Red China, but in deference to the United States, we should seat them in front of the air conditioner.*"

"Out! Out, damned Spot!"

"*I moved to the suburbs for the same reason most family men do—it's a great place to raise hell.*"

"*At one time, the changing of the guard was quite an impressive ceremony.*"

"It's not the beatings, the indifference, the drinking or the philandering, Ernie, it's your breath."

"*So much for our opening remarks; and now, gentlemen, shall we debate the issues?*"

"*There's nothing quite so heartwarming to see as the merger of three giant corporations.*"

"He works much too hard, the dear. I'd feel so much better if he insured himself to the hilt."

"Timmy has to tinkle."

I WILL NOT ACCEPT MONEY FROM THE CIA

"*I feel sorry for her, but I just don't want to get involved.*"

"Somewhere out there is a young lady in flaming-red stretch pants. Get her off the slopes immediately. ..."

"*I've never read anything quite
so moving, and I urge you to accept this offer to
merge with Amalgamated Industries.*"

"Oh, come now. Surely you've heard of socialized medicine?"

"Well, son, you're the man of the house now."

" 'Drag race,' my foot! I know a rumble when I see one!'"

"Mona! You thought of everything!"

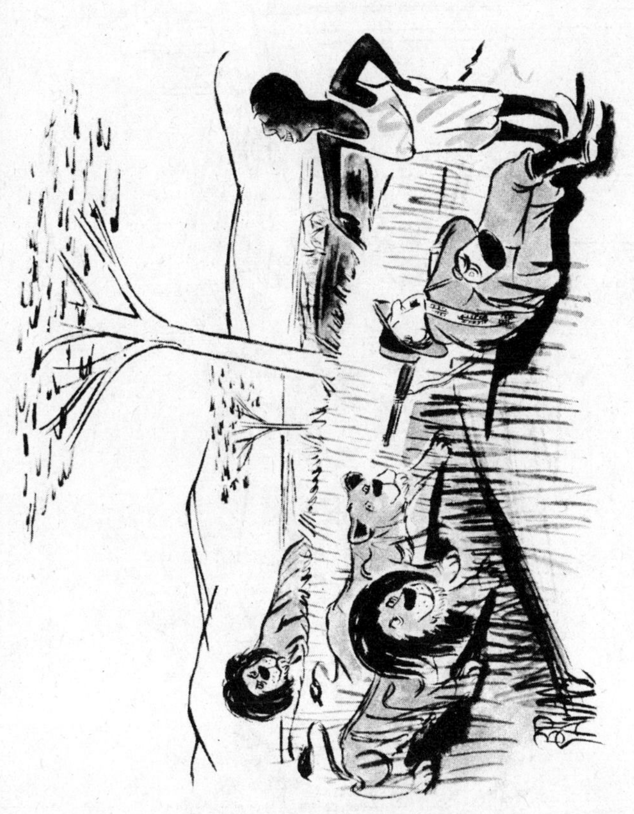

"Watumba! My faithful gunbearer!"

"Like, most chicks couldn't stay me from my—uh—appointed rounds—ya know what I mean?"

"You may show in the union delegates now."

"Two to five years from now, Briggs, we'll probably look back at this and laugh."

"Mind if I sing you a song of the open road?"

"Well, Senator, I think it's time we investigated the State Department again."

"Note the piquant tartness at the first taste, subsiding subtly to a delicate, gracious nuance. . . ."

"The party should be breaking up any minute now. Shall we stay and watch?"

"Oh, look, look at the funny dancing men."

"Great Scott! Isn't that our roving ambassador?"

"Betsy! Say it isn't so!"

"*Guess I'm just an old-fashioned gal, but I want to ask your blessing before I move into Bernie's pad.*"

RECRUITING CENTER
DRAFT GOLDWATER
GO ARMY!
BRIAN SAVAGE

"*Judge Rollins has yet to have a decision reversed.*"

*"It's neither a Nehru nor a Mao.
It's a Father Gilhooley."*

"And yet, as a businessman, I can't help but feel a grudging admiration."

"*Most men lead lives of quiet desperation, but not my Oliver.*"

"*It's from Johnny Carson.*"

"We're living in a sick society
where the traditional values have
become practically worthless . . . the
pound, the franc, the dollar. . . ."

*"It seems to defeat the whole idea of our
conjugal-visiting program."*

"He claims he was only nibbling her ear and attempting to look down her dress. So it's up to you to prove he was cheating, Briggs."

"Wait, how about longhand, then?
Can you take longhand?"

"*Guess I'm just a kid at heart, but **I** still like the clowns.*"

"*This should make an amusing footnote
for my biographers!*"

"Suppose your fellow surgeons found out you lost your nerve at the critical moment?"

"*I don't condone it, certainly, but there's nothing in our code of ethics that specifically forbids it.*"

"*You've simply got to meet Springdale's most eligible bachelor.*"

"God bless the old gentleman.
He simply thrives on controversy."

"Let's talk about your getting time off for good behavior."

"*Any chance of my borrowing the car again tonight, dad?*"

"In case you're interested, we passed
Leavenworth two days ago."

"That's the 'extra something' I was talking about, McCallister, that distinguishes excellence from shoddy mediocrity."

"Betsy, my darling, didn't you get my telegram?"

"Hello, there. I've been wanting to meet you all evening."

"Little lunchie again tomorrow?"

"*Sorry to interrupt the bon-voyage party, but we dock at Yokohama in two hours.*"

"You say you love me. And yet you never want to neck during the prime viewing hours. . . ."

"*Well, another singles weekend at good old
Hotel Point o' Lakes.*"

"I trust you've heard of diplomatic immunity?"

"First we hold free elections, then we establish our
own bylaws, and then, somehow, we've
got to get affiliated with a national fraternity."

"You can always tell an ex-officer by his military bearing."

135

"There's still a lot of little boy in you,
Mr. Brodkin."

"*If you don't pay any attention,
they usually stop showing off.*"

"*Ah! It's good to be home, surrounded
by those who love you.*"

"Toffee, mea, or cilk?"

"This should be interesting."

*"I suppose it was inevitable. Seven o'clock,
'The Wonderful World of War.'"*

"Go home, McCarthy!"

"*What really bothers me is that we're living way beyond our means.*"

"*When I'm required to administer mouth-to-mouth resuscitation, I'm confident that my breath won't offend.*"

"So this is love."

"*Well, at least he's got them agreeing
on something!*"

"Good morning, Fred!!!"

"*You've got to give the cruise director
an A for effort, anyway.*"

*"Business is up 1.37 percent this quarter,
and you ask why we're dancing?"*

"By being the unemployed father of seven, you think you've found yourself a nice little tax loophole, don't you?"

"*My fellow Americans....*"

"Scab."

"*I'm in the advertising game, too! You fellows looking for a couple of nice girls?*"

*"Last year, when you went home to mend
fences—did you break any new ones?"*

"*Newcomers are always so surprised when they find that the suburbs really swing.*"

" 'Sleep tight,' yourself."